THIS JOURNAL BELONGS TO

———————————————————

A JOURNAL IS A SACRED RECORD ...

... a record of your life and thoughts, your ideas and inspirations, your feelings, and reflections.

For many years I used my journal to record stream-of-consciousness writing. I would come to my journal each morning and write whatever was in my mind, without thinking, judging, or censoring, and without stopping. The plan was to do this for at least 15 minutes but most mornings the stream of thought continued for 30 to 60 minutes.

This sort of writing is an extraordinary way to face, clear, and heal whatever is going on in your life. It helps you to process things, big and small, to gain insight, let go and move forward. If you haven't tried this type of writing before, I highly recommend it, and you might like to try it in this journal.

Nowadays, I mainly use my journal to take note of ideas, insights, inspirations, reflections, plans, strategies, objectives, thoughts, schedules, things I've learned, wisdom, quotes, and more. The quotes you will find throughout this journal are from the *Bhagavad Gita*, from the Vedic Yogic tradition that originated in ancient India.

The *Gita* is filled with timeless wisdom on how to walk the upward path – the path of light that leads to liberation, fulfilment, meaning, and purpose. It teaches us to transcend our limited illusory notions of being separate and independent and to expand our understanding to encompass all beings and all existence. It teaches that we are interconnected and interrelated, that we inter-exist with everything else in the cosmos – that we are in fact one and inseparable from all.

The *Gita* contains everything the spiritual aspirant needs to progress on their journey from separation and suffering to wholeness and peace. It addresses the inner struggle that rages between our lower self, or lower nature, and our higher Self, or higher nature – between the forces of darkness and light within each of us – and how to overcome this. It encourages us to orient ourselves towards this higher Self/Soul/God, rather than all the impermanent things of the world that can never truly satisfy us.

The Bhagavad Gita is the perfect antidote for all that ails the modern human. This journal includes a selection of verses from the *Gita* that I have carefully translated into modern, plain language to convey the essence and most valuable teachings of this remarkable holy book.

You can also use this journal with *The Path of Light Oracle* which explores 108 verses by grouping them into 39 essential teachings of the *Bhagavad Gita* and provides detailed commentary and guidance on each.

May the wisdom of the *Gita*, together with your journalling, expand your mind, open your heart, and assist you to find insight, freedom, peace, nourishment, meaning, and fulfilment.

With love and wisdom,

Anthony Salerno

*2.20 The Self was not born and will never die. Existing, it will never cease to be.
It is birthless, eternal, and immutable. The Self does not die with the body.*

2.30 The One Self, inhabiting the body of all beings, is eternal and indestructible.

14.27 The Self (Atman) is Brahman. Eternal, unchanging, and the source of true happiness.

*4.35 Having attained wisdom, they will never be deluded again.
They see themselves in all creatures and all creatures in God.*

4.14 Actions do not affect me as I am not attached to their results.
One who knows this truth does not become entangled by action and is free.

4.17 In order to comprehend the law of karma, one must understand what right action is, what wrong action is, and what inaction is.

4.15 *The wise spiritual aspirants from ancient times who sought liberation performed dutiful action. Follow in their footsteps.*

3.35 Pursuing your own dharma is superior to pursuing the dharma of another, even if successful in such pursuit. Following another's path is filled with danger.

18.45 Through devotion to the work you are called to do, you can attain fulfilment and enlightenment.

6.5 Elevate your self (ego) with the power of the Will. Never let your will be weakened by the self (ego). The Self is a true friend and can help overcome the ego.

2.48 Yoga is evenness of mind.

2.38 Look equally upon pleasure and pain, gain and loss, success and failure as you encounter the battle, and you will be free of suffering.

*2.52 When your mind transcends the delusion of duality,
you will attain the state of holy detachment.*

2.57 Those who remain unaffected by events, neither elated by good nor depressed by bad, neither praising nor despising, are established in wisdom.

3.19–20 Through devoted, selfless service without attachment, you will attain the Supreme. Do your work for the welfare of others and the world.

4.31 True nourishment is to be found in sacrifice and service, and by this means, you will reach Brahman.

5.25 The wise work for the welfare of all beings and attain enlightenment.

3.17 The person who delights in the Self is always satisfied and content. They no longer look to the external world for satisfaction.

*6.20 When the mind becomes still in deep yogic practice, the Self is revealed.
Beholding the Self, the aspirant experiences peace, joy, and complete fulfilment.*

*18.65 Keep your mind on me, become my devotee, worship me,
offer everything up to me, and you will attain me.*

9.27 Whatever you do, make it an offering to me; be it the food you eat, the sacrifices you make, that which you give to others and the discipline and practices you follow.

*3.8 Do your duties. Action is superior to inaction.
Nothing can be achieved through inaction, not even maintenance of the body.*

*2.49 Ordinary action is inferior to action guided by wisdom.
Be ever guided by this wisdom.*

2.59 When the aspirant abstains from sensory pleasures, usually the longing for them lingers. But when the aspirant experiences union with God, even the longings cease.

3.6–7 Abstaining from sensory activities while your mind is still consumed by them will not free you. But by restraining sense activity and performing God-uniting actions, you will succeed.

18.37–8 In the beginning, spiritual practice seems like poison, but in the end, tastes like nectar. Pleasure derived from the senses seems like nectar at first, but in the end, is poison.

5.18 Those who have wisdom have equal love for all beings.

10.10 Those who are devoted to serving me with love for all, gain the wisdom by which they can attain union with me.

3.43 Let the Self/Soul rule the mind and ego and their endless desires.

*2.71 The person who relinquishes all desires born of the ego
and its sense of 'I' and 'mine' realises peace.*

6.29 When consciousness is unified, the yogi sees everything with an equal eye.

6.9 They are a supreme yogi who sees equally family, friends, enemies, supporters, challengers, the virtuous and unvirtuous alike.

12.18 One who serves both friend and enemy with equal love and is alike in praise and blame, pleasure and pain, is well progressed on the path.

13.16 Brahman is indivisible yet appears as the countless creatures.

*7.6–7 All of creation is a product of my dual nature (Purusha and Prakriti).
The birth and dissolution of the entire universe occur within me.
Nothing exists separate from me.*

6.29 The yogi, when consciousness is unified, sees the Self in all beings and all beings in the Self. They see my face everywhere.

6.30 Those who see me in everything are never separated from me.

*10.20 I am the Self located in the heart of all creatures. I am their source.
I am with them throughout and all are reabsorbed into me at the end of existence.*

15.15 I am situated in the heart of all beings, and through contact with me, you can remember and understand.

2.67–68 When you allow your mind to be carried away by the senses, it takes with it your good judgement, just as a storm drives a boat off course. Therefore, go beyond attraction and aversion and abide in the wisdom of the Self.

*4.36 Even if you are the greatest of all sinners,
you can transcend sin by correct knowledge and wisdom.*

*16.2 Practise non-violence towards all creatures. Control your anger.
Do not speak about the shortcomings of others. Be compassionate and gentle to all.*

*10.10–11 To those who are devoted to serving me with love,
I give wisdom by which they can come to me. I will destroy the
darkness of ignorance within them by lighting the lamp of wisdom.*

18.30 Wisdom is knowing when to act and when to refrain from action, what is right action and what is wrong action, what is liberating and what brings bondage, and what brings security as opposed to insecurity.

5.22 Pleasures of the world have a beginning and an end and ultimately lead to misery. The wise do not seek happiness from them.

6.4 When you have overcome desire for sense objects, attachment to results, and have renounced the will of the ego, you will ascend to the state of union with Self.

4.39 Those who have deep faith and have controlled the senses attain wisdom and experience supreme peace.

6.14 With your actions dedicated to Brahman (God), with fearlessness and steadfastness, with the mind controlled and anchored in me, meditate with me as the ultimate goal.

8.14 I am easily reached by the person who continually remembers me above all else.

*13.10 With unwavering devotion to me, the yogi enjoys solitude,
not following the crowd, they follow only me.*

2.22 Just as we discard worn-out clothes and acquire new ones, so the Self relinquishes the body when it is no longer useful and enters a new one.

8.16 All creatures are subject to birth and death, except the one who becomes united with me. For this being, there is no rebirth.

6.43 Once reborn in a new form, the wisdom acquired in previous lives is reawakened, and we strive even harder for Self-realisation.

6.45 Through sincere and consistent effort over many lives, the yogi is purified of all sin and attains the supreme goal of life, union with God.

*2.40 On the yogic path, no effort is wasted, and you cannot fail.
Even a little effort will protect you from the worst peril.*

*16.1 Be fearless and pure of heart.
Be persistent and dedicated to your spiritual advancement.*

6.17 Temperance in eating, sleeping, working, relaxing, and playing is a practice of yoga that will bring an end to suffering.

6.36 Those who lack self-control will find the state of yoga hard to achieve. But those who are self-controlled and disciplined, and who employ the right means, will achieve this ultimate state.

*6.35 The mind is restless, turbulent, and difficult to restrain.
But it can be controlled by the yogic practices and detachment.*

5.21 When consciousness is unified through meditation, you experience abiding joy.

*6.12 Take your seat and strive to still your mind by concentrating on one thing.
The practice of meditation will bring self-purification.*

*6.23 The state of yoga is free from all suffering.
Practise meditation with determination to experience this state.*

17.24 Those who follow Brahman repeat OM while performing their practices, offering sacrifices, and giving gifts.

*9.34 Fix your mind on me, follow me, serve me, love me, and worship me.
Being intent on absorbing yourself in me, you will find me.*

9.29 Those who adore me wholeheartedly live in me, and I come alive in them.

11.53–54 By undivided devotion you can know me, experience me, and merge with me, not by mere scriptural knowledge, penances, or charity.

12.11–12 Surrender your self to me. Surrender the results of your actions while continuing to strive for self-mastery. Surrendering attachments to the fruits of your actions creates immediate peace.

12.17 The accomplished yogi does not avoid pain or seek pleasure, does not grieve or lust after things, and sees beyond good and evil, allowing things to happen as they will.

4.22 That person is free who is satisfied with whatever comes, is beyond the dualities of life, is devoid of jealousy or enmity, and who is equanimous in gain or loss.

2.47 You have the right to do your work, to perform your duty, but not to the fruits of your work. Do not do your work just to get the reward, and do not consider yourself the creator of the results of your work.

*3.25 The ignorant work with attachment to the reward.
The wise work without attachment to serve others.*

3.27 Fooled by identifying with the ego, a person thinks they are the doer of actions. But in actuality, all proceeds from the source of life and its fundamental attributes.

5.8 The person whose consciousness is unified knows that "I myself do nothing," even though they do many things in life.

*4.18 The one who is unified becomes an instrument in my hands.
Even when they act, they do not act.*

3.26 Do not disturb the mind of the ignorant who are attached to action and its fruits. Instead, the wise being should inspire the ignorant to change by right action and selfless service.

16.1–3 These are the divine qualities of your true nature: devotion, courage, truth, love, wisdom, service, kindness, compassion, fortitude, discipline, self-control, temperance, purity, simplicity, humility, sincerity, patience, and generosity. Move past fear, control anger, do not harm anything, study the scriptures, have goodwill for all, and put others ahead of yourself.